My Digital Art

Gemstone Art, By Vijay Simhadri:

Here in the Art Catalogue, I have digital paintings of realistic imagery of gemstones. For instance, there are digital paintings of the following:

* Cut Gemstone Diamond Art.

* Gold & Silver Art.

* Emerald Gemstone Art.

* Alexandrite Gemstone Art.

* Ruby Gemstone Art.

Cut Diamond Sphere & Pure Gold Pyramid:

Rotated Diamond Cube:

Diamond Octahedrons:

Diamond Dodecahedron & Emerald Polygon:

Diamond Pyramid, Alexandrite (Purple) Sphere, Emerald Cylinder, & Citrine (Orange) Cylinder.

5 -sided Diamond Pyramid & Cabochon Emerald Sphere:

Gold, Silver, & Diamond Art:

Ruby Sphere, Gold Striated Pyramid & Emerald Sphere:

Pure Gold Objects above Landscaping:

Silver, Gold Pyramid & Diamond Sculpture:

Silver Sphere, Silver Cone & Gold Sphere.

Diamond Cylinder, Gold Sphere & Silver Cube.

Diamond Polygon & Pedestal:

Golden Arch:

Silver Sphere & Golden Arch:

Golden Pyramid & Silver Spheres:

Diamond, Cut Alexandrite Sphere, Emerald:

Huge Diamond Sculptures:

www.ingramcontent.com/pod-product-compliance
Lightning Source LLC
Chambersburg PA
CBHW050907180526
45159CB00007B/2824